Divorced Virgin, Mother of Two

Divorced Virgin, Mother of Two

Expectations and Reality of Marriage

Marie Duncan-Wagers

Library of Congress Control Number:		2009902690
ISBN:	Hardcover	978-1-4415-2105-7
	Softcover	978-1-4415-2104-0

To order additional copies of this book, contact:
Xlibris Corporation
1-888-795-4274
www.Xlibris.com
Orders@Xlibris.com
57357

CONTENTS

DEDICATION

If ever there is a man who deserves a medal of bravery, it would be my husband. He is a good man, a quiet man, and one who does his best to avoid confrontation. Then he married me. He had no idea what he was in for yesterday and then we have tomorrow.

My son, Seth, who from birth has been taught many of his father's fine qualities and then I added his greatest quality—think like a woman and be a man while you do it. He is amazing.

I cannot in good conscience forget the special loved ones in our home who made this book possible. Each of them contributed a unique quality in their reviews and opinions.

Sam the dog
the greatest pencil chewer and paper retriever a writer could ever have

Soup, Salad, Cucumber, Onion, Kumquat, Crouton, Clover, and Arnold, the turtles
you certainly know when to hold your tongue and not voice your opinion
and
the Hermit Crabs
Easy, Wheasey, Sleazey, and Diseazey
There is nothing that wakes you up quicker than a crab that has an opinion while he is attached to your hand.

REJOICE

When I die
Please don't send flowers.
When I'm gone
And there's no one left to carry on,
Please don't cry over this thing you think of as a loss.
BUT REJOICE!
Don't think of yesterday.
Think only of tomorrow.
Don't think of sadness.
Think of happiness.
Never sorrow.
REJOICE!
My friend REJOICE!
And remember . . .
It's not a loss you suffer,
It's the wisdom we gained from being friends.

In Loving Memory

Jeff Matson
10 May 1959-23 February 2008
A good man, father, and husband.

Beth von der Heydt
16 January 1945-23 March 2008
One of the greatest teachers I've ever known.

Paperback Novel
27 January 1943-1 July 2008
One of the greatest books I ever read, he will be forever missed on my
bookshelf of life.

Mary Ann Carr Ervin
18 September 1924-22 July 2008
A loving aunt, sister, and friend.

Glenna Anderson
5 April 1942-24 January 2009
A loving soul who could find humor in all things, especially reality.

Julia Thal
21 October 1909-21 February 2009
Ninety-nine years of laughter and love that changed the world one day at a time.

Acknowledgment

Many years ago, I knew a wonderful man, and we were the best of friends. Never was our relationship sexual, but it was personal. I thought I knew everything about my guy especially since we had always shared our innermost thoughts. Then one night I was proved wrong. We were about to share our first kiss. We can all relate to that moment when your eyes meet, the gentleness of his touch and lips that are coming together as one. Then he screwed up. He stopped the kiss and spoke.

"I can't kiss you. You're not a virgin."

Somehow my laughter couldn't be contained. I've shared many a first kiss but never one I could compare to dead fish until then.

We sat on the sofa, and my friend and confidant shared a secret he had never shared before. He was a virgin. At least he thought he was sharing a secret.

"I know it may sound silly, but I will marry a virgin. We can't pursue our relationship any further because you are no longer pure," he said softly as he hung his head down in shame. Actually it was more like a sad puppy.

He then continued to dig himself into a deeper hole and kept speaking.

"I will marry a virgin. I will carry her across the thresholds of our home, the home that I built just for her. The home our children will be raised in and one day their children will come to visit. We will be pure on our wedding night as our souls become one. I will be the perfect husband, waiting on my wife as if she were a princess and she taking care of me as if I were a king. She will be the perfect wife, and together we will have the perfect children. That's why I can't kiss you. You're not a virgin."

When he was done speaking, I gazed into his beautiful hazel eyes and burst out laughing. For some reason he took that personally and went home. I understood his need of purity on his wedding night, and I wish I had waited, but it didn't happen. What I didn't understand was where were they going to live afterward. His fantasyland was booked and overflowing.

We stayed friends however. When I moved from Anchorage, where we lived at the time, to the lower 48, we lost contact with one another until that beautiful spring morning when I had the last laugh. A mutual friend telephoned and told me the news of No Lips's upcoming nuptials. He was marrying a great lady. I knew this because I knew her. She was funny, spiritual, kind, loving, and possessed all the glowing qualities of a new bride in search of her Mr./Mrs. Degree.

She also held in her heart his want for purity on their wedding night. Yes, she was a virgin. A unique virgin. An unparalleled virgin. A virgin known to many men on the wedding night. She was a divorced virgin mother of two.

Somewhere, somehow he learned purity did not lie between the crotch, it was also a part of the heart and soul. Close to nine months after their wedding, their son was born. He weighed in at nine pounds six ounces, and he was twenty-one inches long. He was often referred to as a preemie. The old saying "The first one can come anytime, but the second one takes nine months" was definitely true in this case. Over the years they added many children and lived in a nice rented home. And his use of the English language was taken from in-depth conversations to the words, *yes dear*.

It's the simple lessons in life that give each of us the courage to jump the biggest hurdles. All relationships, especially marriage, are stressful and filled with work. However, it is within those endless hours of working together you can build a foundation for your marriage that will last forever. Granted it will have a few cracks, but don't we all?

Chapter One

Garbage Day

Have you ever taken a good look at your neighborhood on garbage day? Sure there are the normal cans filled with trash items like milk jugs, soda cans, and other household garbage; however, have your eyes ever taken mental note of the other items sitting on the curb? A chair, sofa, bookcase, even a mattress, just to name a few.

We live in a throwaway society. When we get bored with something, it is easier to toss it and buy new instead of utilizing other options. Those options may include donating the merchandise to a secondhand store or having a garage sale where you could make a few extra dollars. Granted both of these sources take time, but they would each be beneficial to you and someone else.

The garage sale entails endless hours of effort sorting and labeling, and let's not forget the actual day of the sale plus the cleanup after. Many of us have friends who enjoy putting a garage sale together. And given a month or two, you could even make it a family garage sale—two or three families working together, sharing laughs, and making a few dollars on the side.

Donating is an easy process. Some places will pick up your merchandise. Most want things delivered. Either way you are doing a good thing for someone else in need.

Furniture is not the only thing we toss out as a society. We also toss away values, religion, people, and relationships. Fifty years ago, parents taught their children manners. We often heard *please, thank you, yes sir, yes ma'am*. Simple phrases taught by parents to their children because parents believed it was their responsibility. It was also a simpler time when children didn't chew gum in school and television was still a phase.

The 1960s and 1970s were filled with young people who had found their voices and protested the war in Vietnam, and a new age of drug abuse walked through many families' front door without ever being detected. Even during those times, many parents held firm to their responsibilities of teaching their children manners and respect.

By the new millennium, the computer network had taken over the world. Within minutes you could send a message to someone thousands of miles away and receive an answer back just as quick. Today's society consists of e-mails and cell phones that do everything for you. They can even order dinner for you at the press of a button. In addition to these is the "almighty" text messaging. This is a foreign language of codes developed by rebellious children to purposely avoid communicating with their parents. Recently I saw this firsthand and wondered what has happened to our children today. Two young girls were sitting at the kitchen table of a friend's home and doing their homework. Instead of speaking to each other they were texting the answers. Did they not understand the reason people study together is to get the answers? Times have certainly changed.

You never know where you will be when your cell phones starts ringing. Rings, alarms, instant messaging, and of course those who have to be attached to the Internet on a regular basis. I'm waiting for divine guidance to grace us with the church of mechanical devices. Their eleventh commandment would read "Thou shalt have a mechanical device of communication attached to your head at all times. Amen."

Recently I was in a public restroom minding my own business and doing the same, when I heard a voice from another stall say, "Hi. How's your day going?" I hesitated for a moment before I answered back, "Fine and yours?" Then came the question all women want to hear from a stranger in a public restroom: "How do you feel after giving birth?" she asked. Granted my business at that point was big, but it was not noisy, and I certainly wasn't giving it a name.

It was at that point I realized she was one of those angels announcing the newest church of the land, The Church of Mechanical Devices Stuck to Your Head. You can find them on every street corner and public restroom. Worship only requires a two-year contract from your provider. Quietly I finished my business and waited until she left her own personal phone booth. Then I escaped unnoticed from my birthing chair and out to avoid the many sheep from her fold.

As manners have stopped flowing from a generation's mouth and mechanical devices have begun to grow as appendages, our world has forever changed. Even the family dinner is becoming extinct. I grew up with the family dinner, and every night we had the family prayer. In the time of my childhood, fast food was not as it is today. Families stayed home to eat. There wasn't a hamburger, roast beef, chicken, taco takeout on every corner. Dinner was dinner, and it took place at the kitchen table and began with a prayer. Even greater it ended with each person asking to be excused and then taking their dish, glass, and flatware to the sink. Back then we cleaned up after ourselves. We didn't like it but we did it.

The new version is easier. Jump in the car, drive by a machine, speak to a machine that is speaking to you, drive to window, pay for food, and they will personally deliver it through their window to your car. You can get fries with that also.

With the ability to communicate so quickly from one side of the world to the other, why is it we are too embarrassed to speak to our children about sex? Our daughters are learning about it from experience with lack of birth control, and our sons learn it by hearing the words, "I'm pregnant." In which most reply, "How could you let that happen?"

When I was growing up, it still took two people to make a baby. One thing that will never change is the girl's responsibility for the baby and the shame she feels for getting pregnant so young. And who raises those children anyway? Is it the young girl who keeps the baby knowing full well she has no education, job, or family support and just wants someone to love her? Or is it her parents who did such a fine job with her? Either way that baby will learn what it is taught. If you know love, you can teach it. If you don't, an infant isn't going to teach it to you. It is your responsibility as a parent to teach the child.

Where does the best answer lie in an unwanted pregnancy? I believe adoption. It is a hard road to travel, but so many young couples want to give a child a good home. Yes, there is an emotional burden a birth mother carries with her forever; however, it seems knowing you have given the greatest gift of all to a childless couple should be an emotional bridge you can cross and go on with your life.

Sadly enough, factors like rape and sexual abuse also end in pregnancy. Each situation is different, and each should be handled in their own unique way. Except for the one where the young girl tells no one, and no one cares to notice the extra weight she is putting on, and no one hears her scream as she delivers her baby alone and makes the choice to toss it into a nearby dumpster. This is where society shows its true colors of failure with our children.

—

With everything we toss out, is it a wonder we don't even hesitate to throw our marriages out the door? Some don't even make it that far. They get tossed out the window, and virginity is a thing of the past.

Marriage's end every day with no one trying to find a solution but adding more chaos to the problem. Unions as new as twenty-four hours and old as forty plus years are tossed to the wayside in search for newer, better, and sometimes much younger companionship.

When we leave one relationship and quickly go into another, we tend to take our mistakes with us. I don't know if time heals all wounds. However, from experience I know time helps us to understand why we were wounded or wounded someone else. There are women who get so excited about being in a new relationship they literally sabotage it so they can begin a new one. For some it's an addiction to the excitement of a new man in her life. These woman, enjoy the attention they get from their friends, family and coworkers. They live for the questions about the new man. They become the center of attention and then they begin the adventure into fantasyland.

They are the princess, and he is the prince. She is happy until he does something wrong; and once she finds a fault, she is ready for the relationship to end. The fault must be in him because it is her fantasy. For example, he needs $100.00 for a car battery, and he is little short so he asks her. She loans him the hundred and request a receipt. There agreement is the $100.00 is for the car battery, and he will pay her back on the following payday. Payday comes and payday goes with no loan repayment. When she approaches the situation, he skirts around the questions and cannot produce a receipt for the battery. She makes the decision not to argue about it, excusing the receipt as if he had misplaced it. Later when they are outside, she decides to pop the hood and see if there is a new battery. Surprise, surprise, no new battery. Fault found, she is ready to end the relationship.

He wanted the money for something else. Whatever it was he knew she wouldn't approve so he invented the car battery story. When you loan someone money, they still have the free agency to spend it how they choose. I loaned a friend $1,000.00. He wanted to buy an engagement ring for his fiancée. I didn't just write him out a check, I went with him to the jewelers and saw the ring. The $1,000.00 was just a deposit. The ring cost about $5,000.00. I tried explaining to him if he can't afford $1,000.00, how is he going to afford the payments on $4,000.00? His soon-to-be wife was high maintenance, and at that point he was in love and had no idea what that meant. I thought about it for a few days then loaned him the money anyway. Taking in mind when you loan someone money, you will probably never see it again. And I was right. I never saw the money; however, a few weeks later, he and the fiancée came by my work. I expected to see a ring on her finger, instead the first thing I saw were two gigantic breasts where a flat chest used to be. He used the money for a deposit on her boobs.

All I wanted to do was explode. The ring was never bought. They never married. I never saw my money, and she left my friend for a guy who knew how to enjoy big boobs.

Sadly, our society has now chosen this as an acceptable way of life. No one does anything wrong, and our mistakes are made by someone else. This has lead us to no longer taking responsibility for our mistakes. If we make no mistakes, we pay no consequences. We have made gradual choices to make this society what we have today, and we have passed our knowledge or lack of it to one generation after another. If this sounds judgmental, that's because it is. As human beings, we are the first to judge, first to want, and first to demand instant gratification; and in turn, we have passed this on to a generation of children who want it all now. Imagine a three-year-old with a cell phone and the mother giving it to her. What is a three-year-old going to do with a cell phone? It will obliviously be of no use to her unless her teddy bear and dolls have one too.

We have made great strides in technology, communication, and society; however, in the world of reality in which we will all be held accountable, we have failed. Maybe we should start from the beginning. All hospital birthing rooms and public restrooms, where needed, could have a sign on the ceiling that mothers could read repeatedly as they endure thirty plus hours of labor:

WELCOME TO THE SOCIETY WHERE VALUES, RELIGION, PREMARITAL SEX, AND OVERALL HUMAN KINDNESS IS THROWN OUT LIKE YESTERDAY'S GARBAGE. BUT YOU CAN CHANGE ALL THAT AND MAKE A DIFFERENCE. YOU CAN TEACH YOUR CHILD GOOD VALUES.
TEACH THEM TO RESPECT PEOPLE AND BRING LOVE AND JOY TO OTHERS, AND YOU WILL CHANGE THE WORLD FOREVER.

Sincerely,
The Management

Instant gratification and prestige have become the goals for most Americans. If we can throw out trash, manners, respect, and religion, is it any wonder relationships are no strangers to garbage day?

CHAPTER TWO

Once Upon A Time

When I was a little girl, I loved hearing my mom's voice as she read me the stories of Cinderella, Snow White, Rapunzel, and so many other fairy-tale characters. Their lives were such a mess and then Prince Charming came to their rescue. He knew just what to say and do and became the hero who saved them. Yes, Charming took great pains in finding whose foot fit the glass slipper. Charming traveled hundreds of miles to find Snow and wake her from a permanent sleep. Of course, in his spare time, Charming even rescued Rapunzel from the great tower she was imprisoned in all her life.

"Charming, you are my hero. You saved many a young maiden and rode off into the sunset with each one to live happily ever after."

Wait just a moment!

"Charming, you had your way with Cinderella, Snow White, and Rapunzel. Just how many other women did you run off into the sunset with and live happily ever after'?"

Have you met a few Charmings in your day? Have you learned anything in the process or should I even ask?

Why, as women, are we always looking for our Prince Charming? I do not want the Charming who comes with the mistakes of his past and makes them over and over again. I want the Charming who has learned from his mistakes and is willing to put his ego aside and spend his life with me making all new ones. Of course learning he was wrong and I was right and we live happily ever after. After all isn't that what Charming wants from us? That and someone to clean up after them like their mother.

Keeping those thoughts in mind, let me tell you a fairy tale:

Once upon a time, there was a fair young maiden. Yes, even a virgin. She lived in a simple apartment, and she was climbing the corporate ladder. She was happy, kind, and caring. And every night she came home to a beautiful cat named Fluffy.

The young maiden came from a large family of fair maidens. Each one went out into the world and found their Prince Charming. But this fair maiden refused to search for her prince. She was often heard telling people, "If my Prince Charming wants me, he will have to find me." And so she continued living in her simple apartment, climbing the corporate ladder, and sleeping with her cat named Fluffy.

One evening she arrived home to her simple apartment and was met by Fluffy. The fair maiden noticed the light on her answering machine blinking and so she began to retrieve her messages. The first was her mother nagging her to find Prince Charming. That call was cut short very quickly. The second came from a telephone company offering better rates and service than what she had. Obviously she came to the quick conclusion that call should have come later, some time around dinnertime when she and Fluffy were sharing a can of tuna. It was the third call that sparked her attention. She replayed it over and over again. Could it be true? Was it really him? Had he actually found her as she said he would? She was so overwhelmed. She plopped down into the chair next to the phone to catch her breath. Poor Fluffy screamed in horror as he was squashed for life and would never recover.

The fair maiden made herself comfortable on top of the squashed fur ball and took note of the caller ID. The words *Prince Charming* appeared. She quickly pressed the number listed 1-800-555-3963, which in the future would become the number known to most women who don't live in the real world as 1-800-Screw-Me, and waited for him to answer.

His deep voice took control over her very being with a simple hello. Her heart began to skip beats. She was so nervous her entire body was shaking, and she had no idea she had brought Fluffy back to life. She was oblivious to the real world.

Prince Charming and the fair maiden spoke for hours. They talked of their dreams of marriage and a family, not just a marriage and a family but the perfect marriage and the perfect family. They knew they were meant to be together as one.

Living in the fairy-tale land of Instant Gratification, they began to plan their lives together. Online they found the perfect $300,000.00 home that they would never be able to afford but found a company to lend them the money anyway. It wasn't long until he inserted the Perfect Family software in his computer and began planning the perfect 2.5 children. She wasn't entirely sure of which end of the .5 child she wanted so she left it to him to choose. Of course being the man he would know the perfect thing to do.

She in turn began planning the wedding. Of course the wedding is all about her and the dress. She went to many different sites and found the perfect dress for only $25,000.00. Together they met at a site and picked out the five-carat diamond. The fact it costs thousands of dollars was not important. They would pay it off; after all, it's only money. Of course she picked out the perfect dresses for her bridesmaids and the dress for her maid of honor.

They weren't sure about who to ask to be the flower girl or ring bearer so she looked into her monthly edition of *Brides Are Us* and found the perfect twosome. Charming of course took care of the tuxedoes for himself and his best man. It didn't take long to find twelve princes to go with her twelve bridesmaids.

Together they picked the colors of the wedding, the invitations, flowers, cake, and of course the perfect location for the wedding and the honeymoon. Charming listened intently as she asked his opinion on everything and of course she listened to his. They were perfect because they agreed on everything; and of course, he was perfect because he really cared about the invitations, flowers, cake, and colors like all men do.

While they continued drooling over one another on the phone, she sent out a bulk e-mail announcing her upcoming nuptials. Her life was complete. Many thoughts crossed her mind especially the one about her name. Should she hyphenate her name? The thought came and went. She was more than thrilled to be Mrs. Charming for the rest of her life.

Within seconds, magic dust began sprinkling throughout the fair maiden's living room. Her Fairy Godmother had arrived. The birds were chirping in perfect tune with one another, and her perfect day began. She was magically dressed by the singing birds, and her dress was perfect. She would soon become Mrs. Prince Charming.

Her horse-drawn (poopless horses, of course) carriage delivered her to the majestic church where many knights were there to open her door and escort her on to the red carpet and into the church.

The double doors of the church opened, and the room was aglow with friends and family. The maid of honor and bridesmaids were all beautiful in their one-size-fits-all dress, especially Bessie who wore a size 22. The dress completely covered her big toe. The special-order flower girl and ring bearer looked just like the online picture. The music began, and the fair maiden walked up the aisle as all graceful princesses do. Her eyes met with Charming's, and they were in love all over again. With each step she knew he was her one and only. Of course Charming was gorgeous in his online rented tuxedo. As she approached Charming, he took a few steps forward, reached out his hand, and bowed before his beautiful princess. He took her hand and kissed the beautiful five-carat diamond he would one day lose in divorce court. The online minister, rented the night before was handsome in his robe as he held the official marriage bible.

Their vows were spoken, and tears flowed from the congregation. Then the minister pronounced them husband and wife. They came together as one, and their virgin lips met, and they each shared their first kiss. Charming swept his princess off her feet and swiftly ran to the awaiting grand limo that came complete with a full bar and swimming pool. Together they drove off into the sunset and lived happily ever after.

There is only one thing incorrect about this simple modern-day fairy tale:

EVERYTHING.

Relationships don't happen in a second. They begin with a single attraction, a glance, a conversation, an introduction, and even a smile. Awkward as that sounds in this busy world, it is the beginning of every relationship, even the relationship between a mother and a child. Knowing this, why would anyone believe you could marry and live happily ever after? Everything takes time. Besides, brides, do you really believe your future prince actually cares about the colors of the wedding, the invitations, or the flowers? On an average, one in a hundred actually has an opinion; and since you are going to do it your way, why bother to ask?

Men and women are different mentally, physically, and especially emotionally. God made us this way for one simple reason: One compliments the other. Our society has labeled men to be the superior of the two sexes; and since the beginning of time, women have fought tooth and nail to become equal partners.

Somewhere between better pay and serving in combat, we have introduced our own personal mess into society. This little mess has grown into total chaos, which directly affects the next generation. While Mom and Dad are both working to pay the mortgage on the home they couldn't afford to buy, their children are being raised by day care. I have nothing against day-care providers if they provide the proper day care.

Whatever happened to living within our means? Moms stayed at home and raised the children. Dads went to work and brought home a paycheck. Credit was given at the grocery store by the friendly grocer you've known all your life. It wasn't one of a dozen pieces of plastic waiting to be handed to a stranger behind the counter.

Women were given a special gift of love and emotional strength while men were given the physical responsibility of caring for the family. Of course there are women who are also physically strong and men who possess emotional strength. Nothing has ever been split down the middle and given evenly. Look at Adam and Eve. They weren't equal, but together they were one. And in marriage, that is the common goal, to unite as one.

CHAPTER THREE

Paperback Novel

Many years ago, I met a man whom I fell head over heels in love with. He was a wonderful man. He was handsome, loving, caring, and had a great sense of humor. He had a tender, compassionate side even though he often got tired of bailing people out of trouble because they chose not to think for themselves.

Often employees and friends would come to him for advice and once given the person left with a better, more confident attitude toward the situation. He was a mentor to many people, young and old. He was the perfect listener. For the dozens who listened, there was always that one who also agreed and appreciated his words of wisdom; however, in the span of time, they did it their way. Quickly realizing their diva-in-need performance was not only in bad taste but it was welcomed about as much as a dead fish left in a truck on a hot summer day.

My true love smoked a pipe. The scent of the tobacco made him even sexier. The tobacco had a fresh sweet scent to it, not like a cigarette that lingered on forever. His pipe collection was massive, always clean and always perfect. As any pipe smoker, he had his favorite he would come back to. He was a courteous smoker. This was in a time when people didn't care if you smoked or not. My pipe smoker was so in tuned to people he never needed to ask or wait for someone to tell him they were bothered by his smoking.

During your conversation, you always felt he was totally focused on you, not on other things in the room or what he was going to have for lunch—only you.

One winter morning as we lay in front of a warm fire, he asked, "How would you describe me?"

"You are the perfect paperback novel," I replied within just a second of time.

Slowly he sat up, took hold of his pipe, stuffed it with tobacco, and lit it. The sweet aroma filled the air. I could tell by the perplexed gaze in his blue eyes he was more than interested in my response and why I had come to that conclusion so quickly.

"A paperback novel?" he replied.

"You know the kind the drugstore sells, at least that's how the song goes," I said with a smile.

Together we wrapped up in a cozy blanket and leaned back on the sofa. Then I began to explain.

"Through the years of reading, packing, and moving, the cover of the paperback novel is bent, and the edges are peeling. Some pages are stained from tears you've cried or someone has cried over you. The tears weren't all sad. Many of them came from happy memories, but nevertheless they became stains. Pages are torn and tattered not always due to the pain and hurt you've felt at the time but also to the joy you remembered as you relive the great moments again and again. Tape always seems to bring the pages back together. Maybe they are torn because of bridges you've burned or lessons you've learned. There are even pages with notes written on them. Did something profoundly touch your heart? One never knows, except you.

"Let's not forget the page that came unglued and lost over the years. Was that a chapter in your life you didn't want to remember? A portion or person that was filled with so much hate it scared you to remember it? What about the page or two that was glued back into the binding? Were those pages you learned great lessons from, and they inspired you to become a better person?

"It is these simple observations that lead the next reader of your book to judge a book by its cover. Never knowing who you are, where you have been, or the things you have gone through, only a judgment call by others never knowing the real you. My love, you are the perfect paperback novel."

With those words, we cuddled even closer.

My paperback novel placed his pipe in the ashtray and began stroking my hair. And ever so gently, we laid together once more, making love for endless hours with the sound of the firewood crackling in the background.

We knew we were going to be together forever. There was never any doubt in my mind or in his; we were the perfect couple. We finished each other's sentences and laughed at the same bad jokes. When the cat chased the dog around the house, we laughed 'til we cried. Our hands fit like a glove. We were in love, and that love would only grow stronger with our years. Nothing would change in the life of my paperback novel and me. Our love was perfect; and according to the fairy tale, we would live happily ever after.

After two years of happily ever after, we ended up in separate bedrooms. Mine was in Los Angeles, and he stayed in the Midwest. Sometimes our lives do not always turn out as we expect them to. We are human, and periodically we can all make mistakes. The time we shared together and the friendship we shared forever, neither of us regretted.

Every couple has different ideas about their relationship. What you expect in a marriage is not always what you get. I expected forever. Forever ended in only two years.

When most people asked, "What went wrong?" I simply replied, "I did." I wanted a career, and I loved climbing the corporate ladder. The problem was he was the corporate ladder. We both worked for the same company. With my paperback novel being in an upper corporate management position and myself in a field management position, he was always the boss.

In hindsight, I snapped the shutter of the camera a few too many times. Then he strayed to the arms of other women. Our sex life was never in question when it came to pleasing one another. He strayed because the more I gave to furthering my career the less attention he received. In a sense, I drove him to the destination of the other woman. However, he made the choice of getting out of the car.

It was only after he pulled many strings and I went to Los Angeles, still working for the same company, did I realize how much I loved him and he loved me. We remained close, at least from a distance, and for many years.

Years later, I met and married a man totally the opposite of my paperback novel. My paperback novel had many women and did marry again. I had a son; he lost his. He divorced, and I stayed married. Over the years, we ran into each other at different functions, both personal and professional. It was at one of these functions, I had the opportunity to introduce him to my husband. There was no animosity toward one another. There were a few shocked faces when he and I hugged, my husband not being one of them. He knows I am a hugger, and he knows I would never cheat on him. I introduced them to one another and in what would be to some a very awkward moment was just a normal part of our lives. It was then I realized those old feelings I had were still there. Years later, my paperback novel passed away. It was only then could I come to terms with my long, lasting love for him. He was my first love. He was my paperback novel.

CHAPTER FOUR

Restraining Order

Paperback novel wasn't the only relationship I learned from. There was also Bill. Or was it Bob? Whichever it was, I learned two very important words from that one:

RESTRAINING ORDER

One of my wonderful, dear, single girlfriends set me up with this great guy, Bill or Bob whatever. They told me of his great qualities and charm and most important how handsome he was. For these three women to actually agree on the same man being so handsome was a shock within itself so I agreed to go out on a blind date with him.

After I agreed, they called him and gave him my number. What can I say? I was young, carefree, and stupid. A few days later, Bill or Bob whatever called. Billybob as he will be known throughout history had a sexy phone voice. He was interesting, funny, and very spiritual. I had no problem going out with Billybob sight unseen. I felt very comfortable.

Saturday night, he came over for our date. I had made reservations at this great Italian restaurant about four miles from my home. The food was always delicious, and the atmosphere was perfect for a date. However, the main reason I loved that wonderful Italian restaurant was the ladies' room. Yes, I said the ladies' room. It had a window that opened large enough that even Godzilla could escape gracefully provided she was in a situation where her date turned out to be "the date from hell."

Billybob was quite a gentleman. I remember him helping me on with my coat and opening the car door for me. He drove to the restaurant, again opening my door and treating me like the special lady I felt I should be treated like. He checked our coats, and our hostess seated us at a very romantic table, close enough to the huge fireplace, not far from the ladies' room.

That mid-January Saturday night in my hometown of Anchorage, Alaska, the temperature was ten degrees above zero. The high for the day was eighteen. It was one of those Alaskan heat-wave days. I wore a black dress with a matching jacket and a great looking pair of three-inch spiked heels. My dress was sleeveless so whenever I wore it I kept the jacket on. My hair was curly as always and that night I chose to wear it up. I looked great and so did Billybob in his matching three-piece suit. His hair was dark, and he was very nice to look at.

Shortly after we were seated, our waiter brought over bread sticks and took our drink order. The bread sticks were a meal on their own. They were so soft and delicious, and they melted in your mouth. The evening was perfect so far. The house salad was served in a large bowl, and each person took what he or she wanted. There were three different types of lettuce, tomatoes, red onions, parmesan cheese mixed in a special Italian house dressing. No matter how bad your date was, you would never leave the food behind to escape out of the ladies' room unless . . .

Not since the transformation of Dr. Jekyll to Mr. Hyde has a man changed so quickly. His demeanor transformed from a man I was looking forward to knowing better to that of a dishearten, pitiful, childlike, lovesick teenager. Billybob reached across the table and gently took my hand.

"Marie," he said, "I'm serious I want five children. If the first is a girl, we will name her after my mother. And if it's a boy, we will name him for me." Then he continued to name the other children.

In a split second, we went from actually enjoying a first date to the twilight zone. Then it really got weird. He took out his checkbook and flipped over to the calendar.

"How does April 21, sound for our wedding day? We can wait 'til next April 21. That would give you plenty of time to plan the perfect wedding. The twenty-first is my mother's birthday. That would mean so much to her." Since he was also planning to name one of our daughters after his mother, I knew right then the umbilical cord had not yet been cut.

I kept thinking about my three wonderful girlfriends and the jokes we played on each other over the years. Some of those were outrageous, but never would any of us stoop this low and go this far.

Billybob continued speaking, "I hope all our children are as beautiful as you."

I smiled and replied, "You are such a sweet man." My mouth stopped there. Inside my mind, I was saying, *Move over, Godzilla. I'm using that bathroom window first.* I excused myself politely from the table to go to the ladies' room. Take in mind this all took place before the salad came to our table. Thank goodness Godzilla wasn't there that night. We would have had a major scene going out that window.

The walk home was invigorating to say the least. My feet were sore from walking in the hard snow in spiked heels. Every part of my body was frozen, including my hair, by the time I arrived home. Upon entering my home, I quickly double-checked all the doors and windows to make sure they were locked and I curled up in a nice, warm bed. After I defrosted, I took a warm shower and went back to bed for the night.

The restaurant closed at 2 a.m. Billybob had stayed that entire time waiting for me to return from the escape hatch. About two thirty, the phone rang. Not thinking, I answered it anyway. That deep, sexy voice turned into a sad, whiney puppy ready to cry for his mommy. I told him one of those little white lies that is appropriate to tell when one escapes out of a bathroom window and walk four miles home in the cold.

I said, "I wasn't feeling well. I did ask a waitress to tell you. Sorry, I don't remember which one it was. She must have gotten busy and forgot. Again I'm sorry."
Then he dropped the bomb.
"I'm coming over to take care of you. I can't have the future mother of my children get sick," he said.
"No!" I replied. Thinking quickly, I said, "I might be contagious and then I won't be any good to anyone. Good night, sweetheart." Then I hung up. Ten minutes later, he was ringing my doorbell. I politely told him to go home and that I was not opening the door. After an hour of him talking through the door, I went back to bed. Within fifteen minutes, he left. He phoned upon arriving home. He was concerned.

Other than attending church and telling my still wonderful friends about Billybob and retrieving my coat from the restaurant and getting dinner to go I stayed in my nice warm home and let the answering machine screen my calls. In eight hours Billybob called 112 times. About 2 a.m., he showed up at my front door again. I didn't turn on any lights. I stayed under the covers with a pillow over my head to drown the sound out from the constant ring of the doorbell and a baseball bat beside me for good measure. The doorbell stopped ringing after an hour or two. I thought he had left then I heard the engine of a car running. My bedroom window was next to the driveway. The hum of the engine put me right back to sleep. I guess Billybob was good for something.

I didn't hear from Billybob the next day. Then at 2 a.m., he called and again I answered the phone. "Whatcha doing?" he asked.
"Sleeping." Click.

The next day, a dozen bouquets of flowers arrived in my portrait studio all from Billybob. I love flowers so they stayed. He called later, and we talked about his behavior. And I told him flat out I was never going out with him again, but thanks for the flowers. Three days later, I agreed to go out with him again.

This time we went to a movie. The choice was one of those young and stupid mistakes you learn and never repeat. The movie, *Look Who's Talking* with John Travolta, the reviews were great, and a movie was full proof. Even Billybob couldn't mess that up. He wouldn't dare speak and bother everyone around us; and if he got too chummy, I would just pour my soda in his crouch, accidentally of course.

The movie started. The opening credits were before their time in ways I couldn't imagine, and I loved it. It was a miniature sex education class about the egg and the sperm. Everyone was laughing, everyone, except for Billybob. When he realized what he was watching, he said in a whisper, "Oh, my gosh." At first it was a whisper, and I acted as if I heard nothing. Then he said it again and again. Each time was louder than the time before. Unfortunately, Billybob kept getting louder, and he was now making a scene.
During his amazing three-word repertoire, he slithered lower and lower into the seat, literally sitting on the floor. People were telling him to grow up or shut up. He chose neither. Popcorn was flying, and I moved two seats over. I would have moved three, but I didn't want to sit on the pregnant ladies' lap. Apparently, with all this commotion and patrons leaving and complaining, a soda had spilt on Billybob's lap. Accidently, I'm sure.

I left with a large crowd of people who all received a free ticket for the inconvenience, another ticket for a friend, plus a ticket for the ticket they had paid for. It was actually a great evening. Somehow I ended up with four tickets. The next night, my wonderful girlfriends who did this to me and I went to see a great movie. *Look Who's Talking* was even better the second time around.

Before I got home that night, I stopped by the police department and was quickly educated on what was to become my two new favorite words: *restraining order*.

I never dated Billybob again or went out on another blind date. Unfortunately, it took Billybob over nine months, a few nights in jail, a visit or two, actually ten, from the police, and a special guest appearance before a judge before he got it through his head that April 21 was not a good day for us to be married that year or the following.

This incident took place in the late 1980s. Way before cell phones, the great gadgets we have today, like pocket Mace. One of the policemen who helped me through this situation, and whom I dated for a long time afterward, did a bit of investigating work and found that Billybob was married with seven children.

About a year later, Billybob showed up in my studio. The restraining order had run out, but we had great security, and I didn't think twice about calling them. Before they showed up, he sat down. He had a broken arm. It was in a sling, and it looked very painful. I couldn't help but to ask as I pointed to his arm, "Did your wife do that or one of your seven children?" Before he could answer, security came along with the police and took him away. Never to be heard from again.

Twenty years after the fact, I laugh at this part of my life. However, I was scared. And no matter how much I tried to hide it and not let it bother me, I know I should have handled things differently.

In today's world, I would suggest you never go on a blind date. Meet somewhere at a busy time of the day. Meet for lunch never dinner or cocktails, and never have him pick you up at your residence. If you break rule number one, take one of those great friends of yours with you who set you up on the blind date. Remember it's all right to suffer on a first date when you have a friend with you.

The first date can actually be more fun if you go on a group date. It's more relaxing, and there are so many other people. There is always something or someone to laugh at.

If by chance you use an online dating service, beware. You are typing to a screen. You have no idea what is on the other side of that screen, male, female, rapist, murderer, or maybe by a slim chance, a normal person. I choose to be safe than sorry. Anyone can type what you want to read. The person can type a poem for you and tell you he wrote it, and you have no idea it was written a hundred years ago by Elizabeth Barrett Browning. The Internet is a great way to deceive people.

I have been asked a few times about Billybob and what he would have been like with the modern conveniences of today, cell phone, Internet, etc. He would be a great stalker, better than what he was twenty years ago. What once was harmless years ago could now be deadly.

If for some reason you haven't learned anything from this story, let me leave you with two simple words that may come in handy one day: RESTRAINING ORDER.

Chapter Five

Love is Love.
Sex is Sex.
Love is Not Sex.
Sex is Not Love.

Sex before marriage is a normal occurrence now. The abnormal is abstinence. When the sex hormones start coming out, they really want to make that first stage appearance a great one. For some young men and women, it takes a long time to deal with those emotions. Young men have urges that they need to keep under control. Sometimes this is not easy. It certainly isn't easy if you have never been taught what to expect from those urges. This is why it is so important for parents to communicate with their children on all levels, especially sex.

Girls tend to follow their friends. If one brags that they've gone all the way, they are more willing to go also. Just because one brags, it doesn't mean it is true. When it comes to sex, boys and men aren't the only ones to brag and embellish the story.

Unfortunately even if you are the greatest parent in the world and you have taught your son and/or daughter the ins and outs of sexual behavior, in the long run, they will make their own decisions about sex. Many young girls want to feel loved. By having sex, it becomes love. Sex is not love. Sex is sex. It is an emotion and a natural part of life. Young women tend to become sexually active about age fifteen, some even as early as twelve. They are reaching out for security and truly believe they would find that through sex. This explains the number of unwed mothers we see increase each year. These young girls choose, usually out of peer pressure and the need to feel loved, to have sex. Since they probably haven't been to a gynecologist, they have no clue about birth control; and no young man wants to use a condom. It's not manly. With this in mind, that first-time sexual activity may just turn into a baby.

When you see a gynecologist for the first time, it is awkward and often embarrassing. I've known mothers who have made an appointment for their daughters and told them nothing. Being a teenager is frightening enough; you don't need to add more confusion to a young girl's world. If you have become sexually active, be upfront with your parents. Listen to their guidance. Get birth control and never forget it. Sex is not a play toy you have for a while then toss it for another play toy. When girls and women do this, the proper name society gives them is *slut*. You do not want that title.

Young men and women from religious families are usually taught early about waiting until they marry and share this experience with the person they are going to spend the rest of their lives with. Heed this advice. Sex is a wonderful experience with the right person. Just remember sex is not love. It is just sex.

Parents, mothers especially, need to keep the door of communication open. Teach your sons and daughters abstinence. Teach them that communication, companionship, and the true meaning of love are the building blocks for a healthy relationship. If your parents are too embarrassed about the sex conversation, confide into another adult. An aunt, a teacher, a person from church, someone you can trust and feel comfortable with. Ask their help in speaking with your parents, and if they go behind your back and speak to your parents, don't get upset. They did it out of love because, believe it or not, they were young once too.

We would almost live in a perfect world if couples refrained from having sex prior to marriage. If all young girls said no and held high to their standards, half of the problem would be under control. Ladies, at this point, you do have the upper hand. Just say NO. Your virginity is a sacred gift given only to you. Don't give it away out of peer pressure. I've done many things in this life, but the only thing I regret is that I wasn't a virgin when I married. Please don't make my mistake and regret it for the rest of your life.

Chapter Six

Men Cheat But Women Cheat Better

Before I go any further, I want to make three things perfectly clear.

1. Cheating is wrong.
2. Cheating is wrong.
   And just in case you missed numbers one and two, number three: CHEATING IS WRONG!

If you have chosen to stray from your marriage you are the person who made that choice.

Anyone can argue that "he/she made me do it." However, the bottom line is you made the choice. When the choice of cheating is placed before you and you act on it, you alone are responsible for those actions. What you need to remember is cheating isn't the end of the original relationship. It isn't the beginning of the new. Unfortunately it is the beginning of a decision that you may regret for the rest of your life and a pattern you may never be able to break or control.

Upon entering into the commitment of a marriage, there will be things you learn about the other person you may or may not approve of. Whatever has happened in the past is just that, the past. It was a situation that is done and over. You were not there, and you have no right to judge. Ask questions, make bad jokes, but do not judge. You are responsible for listening, understanding, and being supportive to the facts as you know them; however, judgment is not yours to pass.

Communication is the key to any good relationship. Just imagine a flight of stairs, and you are at the bottom of it. You have just met a wonderful person, and you want to get to know him/her better. Slowly you begin walking up those stairs. That first step may be your first date. It may also be your last. Envision, if you will, the top of those stairs to be an everlasting marriage. With everyone you date, you need to remember he/she is not going to be that person who meets the qualifications of holding a Mr. or Mrs. Degree in your life. They are, however, people. Real people with goals, wants, needs, and a past. Only through communications will you learn about the person you have met, and that takes time. Time is just as important as communication.

Taking the time getting to know someone plus communicating at a personal level plus patience plus understanding plus forgiveness equals A MARRIAGE THAT WILL LAST.

Before a person begins to have a "wandering eye" in their marriage, you have ample time to see the obstacles placed before you. Consider those obstacles or road signs as they appear and face them head on.

You may ask yourself "What are those road signs?" They are simple messages sent to you on a daily basis by your family and friends, sometimes verbal but usually visual.

As you proceed through this chapter, you will have the opportunity to examine three different relationships. Each one will show signs of the need and want to stray from the marriage. Take notes. At the end of the chapter, there will be a quiz. If you have cheated on your spouse, you have already flunked the quiz.

Couple 1:

Jack and Maggie have been married three years. Maggie wants a baby badly whereas Jack isn't that sure yet. Maggie is overcome with the obsession of becoming a mother. Jack enjoys life as it is except for sex. It is no longer an act of making love. It has become the opening-night performance for the biggest entertainer ever, along with a special routine in hopes of becoming pregnant.

Neither Jack nor Maggie wants to start fertility treatments. However, Jack understands Maggie's want for a child, so he agrees to see a fertility specialist. Jack has a low sperm count. The doctor puts him on a regimen of no beer and no smoking. He begins to wear boxers instead of briefs for better circulation. He is a patient man, and he will do this for Maggie.

Maggie must also give up smoking and beer. She also needs to lose weight and improve her eating habits. Along with the vices she has to give up, she also needs to keep track of her monthly cycle and temperature. With the help of the doctor and nurses, they will be able to pinpoint her ovulation schedule. Sex is no longer an option. It can only be done at the right time on the right day, no matter how inconvenient.

Jack loves his wife, and he is taking this very serious. He no longer goes to the bar with the guys to play pool and have a few beers. He and Maggie spend more time together cooking and exercising and enjoying each other's company. After six weeks, they return to the specialist and find Jack's sperm count is doing great. Maggie has lost weight and keeping her charts.

For the next five months, the cycle continues—good food, exercise, no beer, no smoking, and sex only at the correct time. Maggie and Jack are trying to better themselves by doing more things together and learning more on an individual basis. Neither of them sits in front of the television anymore. They work out, take walks, and hold hands more often.

After six months of Jack's sperm count going up and Maggie's weight, health, and attitude toward herself going up, they are actually late for a cycle. Maggie tells Jack, and he is excited. Maggie pees on the pregnancy stick, but it doesn't register as positive. This doesn't always mean it's negative. She could possibly have a low dose of pregnancy hormone in her system still. After two weeks, they see the specialist and do another pregnancy test. The test comes out negative, and Maggie is definitely not pregnant. The doctor assures her this is not a good or a bad sign.

During the next ten months, Maggie and Jack continue on the same track, and they are becoming healthier in every way.

Two of Maggie's closest friends become pregnant. They are overjoyed, and Maggie is overjoyed for them. However, she is also becoming jealous of all the attention they are getting because of the babies. Maggie begins a downward slump. She slowly starts sneaking a bit of junk food here and there, and the weight begins to slowly come back. Then one afternoon on the way home from work, she stops and gets a pack of cigarettes. When she arrives home later that night, Jack smells the cigarettes and wants answers. The words begin to fly as Maggie blames Jack for all the problems, even though he is doing his part. Every month now, Maggie is having her cycle and getting more and more depressed. The doctor has explained other options to Maggie, adoption or in vitro fertilization.

Maggie's performance at work is beginning to suffer as is Jack's in bed. Maggie begins wallowing in her own self-pity. Within six months, her work has suffered enough that she has been written up and given notice. Maggie finally loses her job.

Maggie's frustration has become worse than it was before. The specialist encourages her and Jack to seek therapy. Jack makes an appointment, but Maggie never shows up. Jack keeps his meetings with the therapist and realizes he is not the one to blame and neither is Maggie. Unfortunately, at this point Maggie doesn't want to look at him, let alone speak to him. All communication is shut off. Even though Maggie has sabotaged herself through depression, Jack still loves her and wants Maggie to be a mom. But he loves the woman he married, and he wants her too.

Maggie's two friends have baby showers, and she is not invited to either one because her friends don't want to hurt her feelings. She sinks deeper into depression. The babies are born, and Maggie hears the news through the grapevine. More depression. Finances have taken their toll, and Jack and Maggie no longer participate in many of the sport activities they enjoyed just six months before.

Jack and Maggie are now arguing on a regular basis; and one night, Jack walks out after Maggie blames him for the 1,000,006 time about her not being pregnant is his fault. He drives around for a few hours and then arrives at his favorite bar. Some of the guys are there, and he chugs down a few to numb his feelings. Needless to say, after a few drinks, he begins to look at the waitress the way he once looked at Maggie. Then he makes the choice to cheat. It's only a one-night stand, but he chose to cheat.

Problem Signs:

1. Maggie's *obsession* with a baby was detrimental to her marriage.
   Are your goals the same when it comes to a family? There are other alternatives if you and your spouse can't conceive. Don't close the door to any of those.
2. Of course Maggie *talks to all of her friends* about the baby they are trying to have. These things don't need to be discussed outside of your marriage, especially with in-laws and "outlaws." If you choose to open the door and spread the news, you are inviting opinions. Some people are not always so gracious when giving their opinion.
3. *Seek counseling* early on whether it be through your minister or a professional who deals with this sort of situation. This can be a long hard road, but you need to remember you are in it together.
4. *Blame* is not something that needs to be passed on. Just because the plumbing is in place doesn't mean it works.
5. *Depression* unfortunately does occur with every failed month you don't become pregnant. Don't blame the other person. Enjoy life now and remember you do have other options.

Couple 2:

Frank and Carmen were career-oriented people. They were climbing the corporate ladder of success and doing very well financially. They both loved to entertain and enjoy a lavish lifestyle. Their professional lives allowed them to meet with movie stars, producers, directors, and a few millionaires here and there.

Carmen and Frank traveled a lot. Sometimes after a business "party," Carmen or Frank would take a souvenir home with them—nothing special, just a one-night stand. Over time, Frank and Carmen spent more time with clients than with each other. Their careers and business partners were taking them in different directions. They usually met in the middle for sex.

Cheating had become a regular pastime for each of them. However, neither of them spoke about it and neither had been caught. Until one night, Carmen got caught. Frank came home from a trip and found her in bed with a man. He yelled and screamed. He not only threw a few punches at his wife's new roommate, he also threw all his clothes out the bedroom window.

This caused a bit of concern for a neighbor, and she called the police. Since he was in the public view, literally at this point, and was looked upon as a role model to many, the media had a field day. Of course the police arrived. The newspaper and television crews arrived. And they blamed each other for stepping out of the marriage. Even though they both strayed, neither would take the responsibility for their own actions.

Just like Jack and Maggie, Frank and Carmen lost sight of the vision they began together.

Couple 3:

Mark and Gretchen had both been married before. Mark had cheated on his first wife and placed the blame on her also. However, his version of the story was something like "I loved my wife so much then I caught her with another man. I couldn't stay in a relationship like that so we divorced." He told Gretchen he only wanted a monogamous bond of trust and faith with his loving wife, and that is why he wanted to marry Gretchen.

Gretchen fell head over heels in love with Mark. She felt bad for him because of his first wife. Gretchen's first marriage was shattered because her ex cheated on her. This made her feel empathy for Mark.

Gretchen had many dreams and a bright vision for her second marriage. Mark left the past behind him; and a few little lies he had told to Gretchen, he swept under the rug. Mark had a child from his first marriage, but he told

Gretchen he was not allowed to see her because of the ex-wife, etc. They both wanted children; and when Gretchen got pregnant, they were thrilled. They were doubly thrilled when they learned it was twins.

When the twins were born, Mark helped a lot around the house at first. He was very attentive to Gretchen. After a while, Mark was working longer and longer hours. He really didn't want to go home and deal with bottles, baths, and whatever gift the babies would leave in their diapers for him. Then he began going out of town a couple of weekends a month. Take in mind this had never happened before, and he was not getting extra pay or time off during this time.

When Mark would come home, he was clueless to everything that needed to be done. So Gretchen began giving him directions, and men hate being given directions. One baby needs changing, another burping, now changing, take the trash out, the list was endless. Take in mind Gretchen was new at this also. She was learning as she was going.

Most nights Gretchen would fall into bed out of sheer exhaustion. This did not help the sex life. Gretchen began to catch Mark in a few white lies here and there—next trip out of town, which clients he was going to see, and no extra money for the massive extra work. Gretchen saw many of these red flags because she saw them in her first marriage. She closed her eyes and chose not to look. She refused to see Mark for the true person he was. Her eyes closed to Mark, she put more effort into her children and home.

Then one afternoon while Mark was at work, a young woman showed up at Gretchen's front door. With two-year-old twins and another baby on the way, Gretchen opened the door and greeted the stranger. The young woman politely introduced herself to Gretchen as Mark's fiancée and inquired if he was home. Needless to say Gretchen, who should have been shocked, was actually expecting this moment or something close to it.

She invited Mark's mistress in and told her he would be home soon. Gretchen knew if she wanted answers, she would have to play along. And she did. Anita, the mistress, asked about the babies and if Gretchen had gotten back with her husband. Apparently, Mark told Anita that Gretchen was his sister, and her marriage had gone south. There was no doubt Gretchen was pregnant with number three. She responded, "No, we're not together anymore, and this is what happens when you don't use protection." They both enjoyed the chuckle, and Gretchen knew Anita had fallen for Mark's lies. She also knew if she wanted answers she was going to have to fish for information. So she began her journey.

Gretchen asked how she met Mark, and Anita was so excited to tell her the story. She told her of their plans for the future, including children. Mark loves children. As they were visiting, Mark called. Gretchen was quick, and she would never make another mistake like she had before. Their phone conversation went something like this:

Mark: Hi, honey, are you doing all right?
Gretchen: I'm fine. The babies are fine, and your fiancée is also fine. Mark, you should have told me how lovely she was.
Mark: It's not what you think?
Gretchen: Oh, you have no idea (with sarcasm in her voice and hurt in her heart).

Mark hung up, and Gretchen continued speaking, "Oh, darn, you will be working late. Well, I would love to visit with Anita some more. She is so lovely. Good bye, Mark."

When she hung up the phone, she smiled at Anita; and she knew Anita had no clue what Mark had done and how he used her. Gretchen poured coffee for her and Anita and began to let her down easy with the truth. That was something Mark had failed to mention. She showed her their wedding album and marriage certificate and told her she had seen many red flags of his cheating, but she refuse to believe it.

Anita was hurt, but she felt even worse for Gretchen. She had three babies to raise on her own, and Anita knew it would be on her own. Strange, this does occur during the worst situations in life. Gretchen and Anita found themselves actually laughing at their own stupidity, and there is nothing worse than two women hating the same man and laughing about it.

Gretchen and Anita went upstairs and began throwing all of Mark's belongings out the window, accidentally of course, and enjoying every minute. Gretchen called a locksmith, and they arrived shortly after to change all the locks. Anita decided to sew the crotch opening of Mark's underwear together. She told Gretchen she always enjoyed sewing, and this was special.

The next call was made to the police department. Gretchen dialed the non-emergency number and explained the problem. She wanted to let them know the situation just in case Mark got violent when he came home. The police arrived and were not shocked to see the clothes on the lawn. Apparently, when the call came in to the station, the officer Gretchen spoke with knew Mark from a previous situation much like this one. Apparently Mark was very popular with the ladies.

With a little work, and it didn't take much, Gretchen tracked down the first wife. She lived six blocks away. Mark did tell the truth about being divorced and having a daughter, but it ended there. His ex also had a son. He was a little over a year old. When the twins were born and the sex went south, he went back to wife number one.

—

Oddly enough, these three women got along very well and became good friends. Sadly, Mark was not as happy. The divorce went through very quickly. Apparently, Anita's father was a judge, and he had a few connections of his own. Mark got a second job and was denied visitation to his children. He was ordered to pay alimony and child support and take on all the credit card debt he and Gretchen occurred during their marriage.

Gretchen and wife number one invested in personal license plate holders for their new Mercedes that read "My ex bought this car & it cost only his dignity."

In each of these three situations, sex was a factor. In some relationships, sex is the cornerstone. There are women who believe her man doesn't love her anymore when they no longer have sex. Sex is the way she fills an emotional void. She has the need to feel loved, and the only way that need is fulfilled is through the passion of sex.

One such woman I know slept with her soon-to-be husband before they were married, which is no longer uncommon. The uncommon attribute prior to marriage is virginity. This woman, who I will call Monica, lived with her fiancé for two years before marrying him. When they had sex, she was on top of the world. However, when he wasn't interested, really this does happen in a man's lifetime, she felt as if he no longer loved her.

These emotions continued throughout the next few years of their marriage. In her mind, she believed sex was the only way he could show his love. Fortunately, she was able to communicate these feelings with her spouse, and they sought out counseling. It made a difference in their marriage. Twenty-eight years after the "I dos," they are still married—to each other.

There are signs of cheating that are more noticeable than others. They are referred to as red flags. Men cheat differently than women, oftentimes using the same pattern over and over again. They will often use the same motel/hotel at the same time and day each week, making excuses for working longer hours but never giving you a reason why. Also, he will make excuses for out-of-town business trips that he never took before. But now they are a part of his job, yet he is not getting extra pay or a check for expenses. Has he taken out a credit card in his name only? Check your credit report occasionally, and you will know. Also pay closer attention to the credit card statements. If he was suppose to go out of town for the weekend on business and there is no overnight hotel expense, that is a red flag. Strange calls in the middle of the night? It could be the other woman calling just to hear him say hello.

Another red flag is the cell phone. Check all incoming and outgoing messages. If the usage drops dramatically from the month before, you can usually figure he has a throwaway cell, and you don't have a clue. But now you do.

Surprise him at lunch once in a while. Some women find out the hard way that their beloved spouse hasn't worked at his place of employment for months. If you suspect something is going on, watch for the red flags. Even if you need to hire a private detective to find out. Never accuse him if you are basing your thoughts on your own insecurity. Many women have done this, and the marriage is over because the trust is gone.

Women are not so easy to catch. Very seldom will they use the same motel/hotel more than once. They will drive a hundred miles away from their normal setting, making sure no one sees. She will pay cash instead of using a credit card, and she will always have an excuse waiting if you come across a receipt from a motel/hotel. She may tell you a story about a girl at work whose husband is abusive.

"A bunch of the women put money together to get her out of the situation, and I drove her to the motel/hotel so he couldn't find her car. She gave me cash. I put it on my charge. The motel/hotel needs to have security just in case you trash the room. Another one of the ladies has our friend's car parked in her garage."

Women are more cunning than men. If your wife is a neat freak, she will make sure the house is in order before she leaves and also make arrangements for the children to be picked up at school by a friend. Sometimes her day planner is planned weeks ahead for a rendezvous.

The difference between a man cheating and a woman cheating is not how they think; it is with what they think with. Men cheat for sex therefore he will use his penis instead of his brain. A woman usually cheats because she needs to be appreciated, and her husband and children have come to a point where they take her for granted. When she cheats, it's not about the sex; it is about having someone there who appreciates her. Either way, cheating is cheating. If you make the choice to walk out of your marriage box and cheat, just remember you are the one who chose to walk. You can't blame it on anyone or anything but yourself.

If you do get proof on your cheating spouse, do not go out to dinner and confront him. The money you spend on an extravagant dinner, which will be flushed down the toilet, you are going to need for an attorney. Remember don't jump to conclusions. Get your facts in order.

My husband is a good example of working long hours. He is a CPA and with his career choice, there are many times of the year that are busier than others. At the end of each year, his office mails paperwork out to all the clients. That paperwork needs specific information from the previous year, and every year tax laws change. No matter how sophisticated your computer system is, this still takes time to get done. Remember he has to do these things in addition to his regular responsibilities. Simply put, he works more hours. January 1 through April 15 is a busy time of year. He works twelve plus hours a day and six days a week. During that time, I am a tax widow; and I take care of things he normally would because of it. Don't forget the fifteenth of each month from May to December is also a deadline.

During these times, he doesn't have time to take of car maintenance, he doesn't like to anyway, car licensing, or home projects. He will miss a few school concerts, etc. However, our son, Seth, knows he is working; and this a just a busy time of year. There are times when Seth misses his dad he just needs to have daddy time. Sometimes they will play a board game or go out to dinner or just watch a movie together. Children need this time. I also know I married a man who is loving, caring, and honest as the day is long. He would never cheat, and I would never cheat on him. We made a covenant with the Heavenly Father to be married not just for time but for eternity. Together we became one, and together we will stay one. Our marriage commitment is the cornerstone of the foundation of our marriage. I'm so grateful I have the loving husband I do.

CHAPTER SEVEN

Take the Trash Out, Please

One hundred men and one hundred women were surveyed and asked to rate the importance of "How your spouse can show you love."

They were given five topics:

1. Taking out the trash (without being asked)
2. Sending flowers
3. Sex
4. Jewelry
5. A night of romance

The one hundred women surveyed voted as follows:

1. Trash: 38 votes
2. Romance: 28 votes
3. Sex: 14 votes
4. Flowers: 12 votes
5. Jewelry: 8 votes

The one hundred men surveyed voted as follows:

1. Sex: 82 votes
2. Romance: 10 votes (Planning a romantic night with your wife is a guaranteed night of sex.)
3. Jewelry: 8 votes

Trash and flowers got a lot of laughs.

Women and men have different emotional and physical needs. While the number one answer was having her man take the trash out without being asked, a night of romance came in at a close second. Both show love and fulfill an emotional and physical want, need if the trash smells bad. Many women show their love by word and deed. If your wife comes at you with a meat cleaver she is not showing love.

For the one hundred men surveyed, when the word *sex* was mentioned, that was their number one choice. Most felt flowers were a waste of money, and jewelry was good if it came in the shape of a Rolex.

When I took this same survey to a group of one hundred young couples, all of the men replied with sex as number one. They didn't listen to anything else. They obviously didn't need to. Eighty of the women wanted a night of romance. Twelve wanted jewelry, and eight wanted flowers.

I took the same survey to a group of one hundred married older couples. The men agreed sex was great, but as one man said, "You get it when you get it and enjoy it." Seventy-six men chose trash. Over the years, they have taken it out all the time so now it was her turn. A night of romance came in with fifteen votes only if they didn't have to wear a suit and tie. The other eight men marked whatever their wives told them.

The women could really care less about all the topics. They've had the sex, the thrill of the trash dumping, flowers, jewelry, and romance. All they wanted now was to spend time with the man they love, and of course this means they would have to listen.

During our lives, our priorities change. We no longer have the same wants and desires of a sixteen-year-old at the age of fifty. Those were wonderful, carefree days; but now we are looking forward to those golden years and grandchildren.

When two people marry, the objective is to unite for love, forever. Sex is an added bonus to the relationship, the ice cream on the cake, if you will. Sex is an emotional passion two people share, but they are not defined by it. The emotional outlet has a dynamic appeal, but their love is not solely based within its boundaries. The couple who marries for love enjoys each other's companionship in ways additional to sex. It's through that intimacy couples continually discover the unique qualities that brought them together in the beginning.

CHAPTER EIGHT

The Marriage Box

Marriage can be compared to many tangible items. I sometimes compare it to a box. Your box has four walls. Each wall is solid and attached to another. You may want to add windows and curtains, but whatever you choose, your box is your box.

Inside your marriage box is a spouse, children, in-law/out-laws, financial responsibilities, and many other items of importance.

/	I	SPOUSE	M	/
/	N			/
/	N		O	/
/	L			/
/	L		N	/
/	A			/
/	W		E	/
/				/
/	S	CHILDREN	Y	/

If you stray outside of your marriage box, you hurt everyone and everything within its boundaries. Your spouse will feel pain, hate, and bitterness toward you. The in-laws are going to hate you because you hurt their baby girl. By the way, it will always be your fault from this point forward. Also, men cheat more than women.

Studies have shown children of divorce, which is the direction you will be headed when making a decision to cheat, have marital and commitment issues. They are three times more likely to divorce than the national average. Depending on the situation with a divorce, most states grant joint custody, with the children living with the mother. There are cases where the father has custody and the mother only has visitation. The oldest child is usually the one that becomes the mom's sounding block. This is especially true if the child is ten or older. Girls tend to hate their fathers and blame everything that goes wrong in their lives on daddy. Boys grow up hating their fathers and looking to another man as a father figure. When these boys grow into young men, they face commitment issues that lead to literally being scared of a mental and physical relationship because the father figure they should have had and maybe never found was never around to teach them the example of being a husband and a father.

The financial responsibility is a story beyond words. The judge is the one who chooses alimony and/or child support. In some state, both are granted and in others you have a choice. Take in mind you will also lose everything you have ever worked for. However, you are left with a few things, dignity not being one, and you have the opportunity to knock at the front door of the home you once owned to pick up and drop off the children who once greeted you with bright, happy faces at the end of a long workday. That's something to look forward to. One of my favorites is the feeling of rage you will be consumed with when you see that she has gone on with her life, and you are still sitting on your pity potty. That feeling usually hits when her new boyfriend answers the door of the house you used to own.

Those school conferences you once attended together? Not anymore. That only happens in the movies. Your ex will be more than happy to tell your children's teacher(s) what kind of person you are and probably embellish a bit for good measure. Have I mentioned everything is your fault? It is and it always will be. If you and your wife divorce when your oldest child is in kindergarten and decades later she is failing a class in college, that too will also become your fault. The fact of the matter is everything is your fault because she will never admit to any of the blame. Women tend to be hateful and carry a grudge for long periods. Consider forever a long period of time.

Therapy is often encouraged after a divorce. There you will have the opportunity to work out many problems like cheating, accepting responsibility for your actions, and learning how to control that new tick in your eye that begins twitching when a phone rings and you are scared to death it's her.

The answer to avoiding all these problems and more is DON'T CHEAT. Seek counseling, be willing to change, and remember why you fell in love. All marriages have hurdles that need to be jumped. Keep the communication open and honest, and you can jump those hurdles, no matter how high, together forever.

CHAPTER NINE

Speed Dating
Vroom, Vroom

Time is what makes a relationship work. Recently I attended a speed-dating seminar. My husband and I have been together fifteen years, and he had been patient as I did my research. However, for some reason he was not very happy with me dating other men. Technically it was only an eight-minute date twenty times over, but he still wasn't happy.

Speed dating has been around for a few years now, and the concept is the same whether the program is run the same or not. Usually classes are advertised through the newspaper (check the singles column), and you need to make advance reservations.

When you call, you need to get the date, place, time, and cost. There will be a cost. The people who run these programs are either professional matchmakers who do run a legitimate business or they are professional scam artist. Either way you will need to make a deposit to secure your placement. Do not give them a credit card or send them a check at that time. With the information you asked for upfront—date, place, etc.—you need to make a few more phone calls. Usually these are held in a hotel conference room. If it is being held in a private suite of a hotel, think scam. Call the hotel and confirm the information. Speak with someone in management and ask specific questions:

1. Has this company used your hotel before?
2. How many times?
3. Do many people turn out for their service?
4. Just between you and me, if a person showed up without an appointment, do you think they would let you take part?

If this company has never used this hotel and you are leery, in which you should be anyway, call the Better Business Bureau. They will have more information that will be helpful.

Once you have found the business is legitimate, you can choose if you want to make reservations. Just remember, even if the business is legit, they may not show up; and they have your credit card number.

When I phoned and made reservations, after the background check, I told the woman I didn't use credit cards. She went ahead and put me on the list; however, if she had other clients who confirmed and paid, I would be bumped off the list. At that time, I was first on the no-pay list. A few days prior to the course, I called to confirm. The class wasn't full so I was fine. The day before, she called me to confirm, and space was available.

At that point, I was honest with her and told her of my intentions. She understood and agreed to my coming. You do have to show ID to prove who you are, but that information is not released unless you request it. She changed the name on her list to Samantha (after my dog) Johnson.

After arriving, I filled out a simple questionnaire and paid in cash. She was very legit, and I do believe she just wanted to help people find that special someone. Each participant was given a name tag with the first names only. She kept her classes small—only twelve to fifteen couples. Through research, I've found some of these classes are as large as forty couples.

The seating arrangement consists of a few long tables with chairs on each side. The women stay seated, and the men move at the proper time. Each person is given a sticky notepad and pen for notes, and they can choose to give their phone number anytime.

With the ring of the first bell, the woman has eight minutes to ask the man questions. At the sound of the second bell, the man asks eight questions. The third bell rings, and the couple can freely talk and answer questions for ten minutes. If you want to give him/her your number, you can at that time. At the sound of the next bell, your date is over. The man moves to the next seat over, and another date begins.

If you're not sure what to say, ask direct questions:

1. Have you ever been married?
2. Divorced?
3. Children?
4. What do you do for a living?

These are basic questions that will give you a clearer picture of the person in front of you. Take in mind most men and women who are taking this course are desperate for attention, which means you will be hearing a lot of bull before your time is over.

Dave was my first date. I could tell by his body he did construction work. He was handsome and very personal. He, like the rest of us, felt out of place. I glanced down at his hand and saw a white line where a wedding band would have been. His tan was dark; however, the ring site was white as if he had just taken it off. This indicated three things:

1. He is still married and wants action on the side.
2. He is recently divorced or widowed.
3. He is also writing a book on relationships.

Quickly, I concluded he was not writing a book. He also didn't have that woe-is-me sad puppy look of most divorced men who have lost everything or the pain and agony of losing a spouse. My first question:

"How long have you been married?"
"Seven years," he replied.
NEXT!
It took him a second before he realized what he had said.
"How did you know?" he asked.
"Your ring or lack of it," I replied.

I took advantage of my question time and asked what was happening in his marriage. We spoke in only whispers. I didn't want anyone else to know about his situation because he made a mistake by coming. He just needed to talk to someone, and I was the lucky someone. We spoke about his wife and his feelings. It didn't take long to get to the heart of the problem.

We went through our time, and I realized he was a good man. He truly needed to speak to someone. I gave him the number for a therapist, and when our time was over, he left. Before he left the conference room, I saw him return his wedding ring to his hand. At least something good came out of that day.

The next few hours I sat there with a frozen smile upon my face, listening to some of the greatest lines of bull I've ever heard. However, through it all, four men gave me their phone numbers. I've never considered myself dating material even during my dating years; however, it was nice to know there were men in this world who looked beyond my height, from side to side, and saw something better.

We live in a society where looks are everything. You can't be fat or too skinny. Your hair needs to be perfect at all times, and heaven forbid if your mascara gets smudged in public. The only thing worse would be to break a nail and not have a file. What is this world coming to?

None of us is perfect. And what is perfection anyway? We compare ourselves to movie and television stars and models, and as women, we compare ourselves to all women. There is no perfect look. We are all beautiful in our own way. There are those who judge people by an outward appearance. You have to look beyond their ignorance and understand you were made like you are for a reason.

If you choose to speed date or anything similar, it's important to remember a few important points. When you give your number to a man you have never met before, you are inviting a future stalker into your life.

The packaging may look great, but you know nothing about him. He could be a serial killer, a thief, or just mentally unstable. You don't know what you are getting into. My advice, after living through a stalker, is get his number, and you take control of the situation.

If he gives you his number, think about it before you call, usually a week. Never agree to a first date until you've spoken on the phone a few times. This is another week. You can block your number from showing up on his caller ID.

When and if you decide to meet, do it in a public place during a busy part of the day. Sunday brunch is good or lunch on Saturday. Avoid bars and dinner. You can also go for a group date. Movies are good, but there is no interaction. Bowling is a great way to see how people interact with one another. If you can laugh at yourself as you go flying down the alley with the ball still attached to your hand, it is a good sign you have a great self-esteem, and you can handle more than you think. Bowling does have its good and bad points. You know he is going to check out your backside. That is the bad point, but the good news is you are checking out his. If you can check it out and not break out in a session of point and laugh, you may be on to something good.

—

CHAPTER TEN

Measuring Time

Somewhere between reading paperback novels and restraining orders, I realized you don't need to jump in bed on the first, second, or twentieth date. How long should you know someone before you marry, kiss, or sleep with him or her? The unwritten rule of society is a good-night kiss on the first date or you can be labeled a slut and sleep with him on the first date. Parents, your job is more important than you think. Morals begin early in life. Teaching your children good morals is important, and with your teaching, you also have to set an example. If you are married and you choose to stray but you've taught your daughter she needs to stay pure, don't be shocked if she doesn't.

Granted no matter how much you teach your children about sex, they will always make their own choices. However, if you don't teach your children about sex, they will get their experience somewhere.

Getting to know each other is a simple process of speaking and listening. It is called communication. For those of you who have no idea how this works, let me enlighten you. Your words and his words meet not on a computer-screen chat room but in the real world. You laugh, he laughs, and you begin to get to know one another. This type of conversing has been going on since the beginning of time. Adam and Eve did it and so far so good.

Speaking and listening is the only way to get to know the other person. Happiness, sadness, love, hate, frustration, and basic human kindness are emotions that make us unique. Sex is an added bonus in marriage, not a reason to base your love on.

Imagine, if you will, all couples not having sex before marriage. All right, now I'm living in la-la land. No fairy godmother could pull that off.

Men and women I interviewed for this part of the book were placed in two different categories. The first being those who slept together then married. They had more disagreements and often a fairly shallow relationship. Their expectations were based more on a material world. Finger-pointing blame slowly became the common bond of their soon-to-be short-lived marriage.

One hundred people participated, and ninety-two of those one hundred were divorced before they celebrated their seventh anniversary. Eighty-seven of those people blamed the other person while thirteen actually took some responsibility for their actions and admitted to it.

The second group of one hundred people waited until their wedding night to have sex. Ninety-two of those people were held to a more spiritual plane. Eight of them were older and had no religious affiliation. Nineteen sought out therapy during their marriage and four of the one hundred divorced, three of them between the tenth and fourteenth year of their marriage. This group also included fifteen individuals who had been in previous relationships and chose not to have sexual relations until after they married.

In any marriage, respect is a lifeline, and you need to give it. The broader the bond of communications, the more the two people compliment. one another. Even though each of these situations was different, the only common link was sex prior or after the wedding. All of the people interviewed expressed their personal sentiments of urges. Those are normal, and every man in the second group confessed to taking a cold shower or two.

CHAPTER ELEVEN

The Commitment

You have found the woman you want to settle down with. You know she is perfect in every way. She hasn't seen your flaws, and you haven't seen hers; and if you have found a flaw with her, never, and I mean never, point it out. It's not healthy. She may throw something at you.

You have planned the perfect proposal, and it was just that. Perfect. You are now engaged, and you haven't got a clue of what your life is going to be like after you say I do. Before you get to the "I do" part, there will be certain rituals you will have to endure, I mean enjoy. Since you are at a stage where you are still listening to each other, this is much easier. You will be meeting extended family. Take in mind she is meeting yours also. You will both have skeletons in your closet. Deal with it. Laugh when you can and cry when no one is watching.

You may have an old girlfriend show up unexpectedly at one of these affairs. She wants to see what you are settling for, and she wants to show you what you could have had. The joke is on her. You aren't settling, you are marrying the woman of your dreams, obviously not the past girlfriend of your nightmares.

The same may go for her family. An old boyfriend may just pop over to say hi to the family. Of course he knows you're there. The entire world knows where you are. You are meeting the family. The mother of the groom enjoys getting the family albums out and showing off your fiancé in his younger days. You will hear how cute he was and of course that little slip of "You two are going to make beautiful babies. Oops, I can't believe I said that out loud."

Who knows what the mother of the bride will do. They are always unpredictable; however, if you are meeting the father of the bride for the first time, don't be surprised if he hates you. You don't have to do anything for the father of the bride to despise your very being because no one is good enough for his little girl. There is no Prince Charming out there who loves his precious baby girl more than Daddy does. Don't screw this up. Daddy needs to know you can take care of his baby girl forever. If you can't, he will be the first one to tell you.

Along with the family comes the showing of the ring. Hopefully, you have used common sense in choosing the engagement ring. You have purchased something in your immediate price range. Never purchase that expensive ring that is equal to the down payment of your home. You do not need to get deep into debt before you even say I do. What is important is she loves it. You can always upgrade the ring in years to come. You can also purchase it later. Nothing is written in stone that says you need to place a ten-carat diamond on her hand. Be sensible about finances from the very beginning. This also includes the wedding plans.

Do you want a small wedding or large? One best man and a maid of honor or a dozen? Do you have the common sense to plan this yourself or do you need a wedding planner to think for you? Where do you want to go on your honeymoon? Can you afford a honeymoon right now? These are things you need to think about when planning a wedding. One thing you need to keep in mind is your wedding is one day of your life. Your marriage is forever. If you go into debt and spend $25,000.00 on your wedding, that is a bit extravagant. That is a good chunk of money you could put down on your first home. And how much of that did you have to charge? All very important questions, and now you get answers from a professional photographer who has been to those $100,000.00 weddings and those $500.00 celebrations.

Not everyone can afford to pay $20,000.00 for a dress. Granted it's all about the dress and you on your day. Everybody else is just there to make you look even better. Of course, there are invitations, portraits, flowers, cake, reception, food, tuxedoes, gowns for the maid of honor and bridesmaid. If the wedding is outside, you will also need a large party tent for that, just in case rain that wouldn't dare show on your wedding day.

Now a few more things to throw in for good measure, favors for the reception, candles, hair for that special day, not just for you but for your maid of honor and bridesmaid. Don't forget the perfect manicure and a pedicure if you are wearing open-toed shoes. That reminds me you need shoes for your dress. Besides the regular flowers at the wedding, you will need a bouquet, and the men will each need a boutonniere. As will your fathers and your mothers will need a corsage. Almost forgot, where are you going to have it? If you have it in a park, you may have to get a permit and pay a fee for the park area. The minister? Personally, I feel they should marry people for free; however, they don't. Will you be charged for the church and reception area? Do you want alcohol at your wedding? It's best to save that for the marriage. You are gonna need it when you see the cost of your wedding.

The dresses for your maid of honor and bridesmaids come out of your pocket. Do not expect them to pay for them. Also the shoes that go with the dress, that fairy godmother just waved her wand for those. Fittings for the dresses are usually extra, and remember one size does not fit all. Cousin Jeanne may be a size 6 and have the perfect features to pull off the strapless gown. However, Cousin Hilga is a size 22, and the thought of wearing a strapless gown is not an option. Remember if there are children at your wedding, they could be scared for life. We are talking a lot of therapy for some child.

Here are a few suggestions for the dresses. Find a color that all of your ladies in waiting look good in. Then choose an individual dress style for each of them. These dresses are an investment, so be sensible and get something they can wear again. Instead of a long dress, go with short. Shop around and find a seamstress to do their dresses. You can save a lot of money there and still look beautiful.

Your gown has to be perfect. If it is not perfect, don't bother to show up for the wedding. Remember it's all about you anyway. By the way, how many times are you going to wear this gown? Once. By the slim chance twice if you are lucky, and there is a second reception planned for the other side of the family who lives ten thousand miles away. Even if you mess this marriage up and marry again, you will get another dress. I have seen brides spend $40,000.00 on a gown they wear once. At the reception, she and her husband smash cake into each other's faces, and the gown gets the brunt of it. The cleaning of this gown can range anywhere between $75.00 to $500.00. It depends on the fabric, detail, and cake you chosen. Years ago, the idea was to be able to pass your dress on to your daughter. What if you have all sons or no children at all? That dress will grow old with time. If it is not stored properly, it will turn yellow. This is just a fact of life. If you do have a daughter, the odds are her being the same size you were on your wedding day are fairly slim. However, for the sake of argument let's have the dress fit perfect. The odds of her wanting to wear an outdated style of dress are very close to zero. However, the veil is a different story. A veil can be revamped to fit almost any dress. That is an heirloom to pass on. Remember we are raising our children in a material world. They want and you give. The wedding won't be any different.

Most brides are not aware they can rent that same beautiful gown they want at a fraction of the cost. Invest the money you save into other things. Portraits are a must, and they need to be professional. This is not being cheap. It is being practical.

Who is paying for the wedding? Mom and Dad, Mom and Stepdad, Dad and Stepmom? What about if you and your fiancé have lived together for a year or two before getting married? Should parents still pay for the wedding? All good questions and the only thing I can tell you is nothing is written in stone when it comes to a wedding, except the people who wait on you hand and foot want to be paid, and your check better not bounce.

Now you are ready to plan your perfect wedding. You and your fiancé set the date. Most couples set it for a special occasion, first date, first kiss, even the first time you held hands. The date is set. You decide one year from the day he proposed. Now you start making your plans.

Are you going to hire a wedding planner or take on this project yourself? Wedding planners are wonderful if you can afford them. Again, for the sake of argument, let's say you can. Even though you are going to use a wedding planner to do all the work, you have to find the perfect wedding planner to work with. This may take several appointments to find the person you can work with and one you can afford.

Finally, after six weeks, you have found the perfect wedding planner. He is great, and he has been doing this for years. A wedding planner can be a man and not be gay. Some men have a sense for organization and flair. Mr. Wedding Planner is arranging the wedding destination. You decide on a large formal church wedding, but your fiancé wants a small outdoors wedding. Large formal it is because it's your day. Next, how many groomsmen and bridesmaids. You want twenty of your closest girlfriends, a flower girl, and a ring bearer. He wants a best man. Since it's the perfect wedding, both sides need to be equal. You win again.

As the planning continues, you will ask your fiancé his opinion on just about everything. You will only listen to your wedding planner because he knows everything. You will ask about the invitations.

"Honey, do you like this off-white or this slightly off-white?"

"Honey, do you like the white or real white for the ribbon?"

"Honey, do you like this cursive font or the cursive font?" (Take in mind nobody can read the cursive fonts because there are too many squiggly lines, and they all overlap each other.)

Men, during this time, you will be asked for your opinion over and over again. Just remember it doesn't matter what you want. It's her day.

Flowers are the must at any wedding. Have you ever noticed flowers are sent for funerals but no one sends flowers for a wedding? The living have a much better chance to enjoy them than the dead. Have them delivered a few days before the wedding to the bride's home. This makes for a wonderful surprise.

Gentlemen, you will have an opportunity to choose the tuxedoes. She will keep this very simple for you, and your choice will usually be black or black. Try not to get the two confused. She will ask your opinion on just about everything, but again remember your fiancée and the wedding planner will make the decisions because it's her day.

Sure your opinion will count somewhere during the process, but in the real scheme of things, just remember it's her day, and you are just along for the ride.

Closer to the wedding day, you will be doing the cake and food tasting. Within the first hour of the cake tasting, you will learn there are ten different types of chocolate, at least six types of vanilla, and the list goes on. Pay attention and narrow it down to two. Make sure one is the one she likes. If you say you like one type, she will choose the other. I have no idea why women do this. We could have been born this way. It may be a genetic disorder that began with Adam's rib being inserted into Eve.

Now let's go to the gift selection. Years ago, you sent out your announcements, and the guests decided on what they wanted to give you. Today's modern bride does all the thinking for you. She and her husband will go to a few fancy places and register. They will choose the china pattern, and you can add to it—kitchen appliances, crystal, big screen TV. Lucky you, you get to buy something from their list. Most modern brides want it all when they marry. Some have common sense but most don't. Men, you will be dragged along for this shopping expedition and enjoy looking at china patterns.

After all is said and done, the day is finally here. Sure you have second thoughts and a jittery stomach. We all do. Men and women combined. You may have chosen to write your own vows or just say the traditional ones. Now comes the moment you've waited for. She walks down the aisle, and she is beautiful. All those choices you were asked about? They don't amount to anything when you see how beautiful your bride is.

This is your day. Remember it forever. If more couples do, they would never divorce. Marriage is a sacred covenant made between a man and a woman under the eyes of God. The three of you are in this together.

The reception is over, and the limo awaits. Your life together has now begun as man and wife. Every path you take will not be easy to follow. Many couples let the man lead; other couples are happy with the woman leading. The one thing you need to remember is in a marriage there are no leaders. You walk hand in hand. You are each other's rock, each other's forever partner. And pray you always have the communication skills to make it through the rest of your lives together.

The Man's Survival Guide to Sanity

Attention all men:

Are there days when you are totally clueless on why your wife is mad and why she won't speak to you? Then this section was written just for you. You are hereby given permission to copy this portion and keep it with you at all times. Good luck.

By now you have met a wonderful woman, and your relationship is in full swing. You may have even married her. Congratulations. As you get to know one another, you begin to understand those special things that made you love her and those cute little didn't-annoy-you-then-but-they-are-now things that you can't stand anymore. Don't worry. She has a list for you too. However, for the sake of argument, I would suggest you never speak of her annoying list. At least, in this lifetime.

Women don't always say what they mean, and the reason is clear. They want you to read their minds. Again, good luck. This is not a normal human practice; however, for the sake of argument, let's just say you can. And for those who can't follow along, take notes.

A woman has certain tones. For example, a loud sigh is not a word; however, it speaks volumes. This nonverbal statement you will hear often in your relationship when you are not reading her mind means you screwed up. You are just short of a moron. In her eyes, you are an idiot. The loud sigh comes out, but her innermost thoughts, which you should be reading by now, are saying, *Why am I wasting my time arguing with you? As always I am right, and you are wrong.*

You can follow her loud sigh with a *what* and a look of stupidity, or you can save time and effort and do one of the following:

1. Admit you are wrong. When doing so, this only makes her more right, but just because you say it does not mean you actually mean it. Trust me on this one. We will cover it later.
2. Admit she is right. Say something like "Oh, wait, I understand what you're saying. I apologize." Then listen to everything she is talking about and act interested for a long period of time.
3. Do nothing and sleep on the couch. This will get you no sex for a week. I suggest number two just in case you are still wondering.

Next on the list are the W words:

Whatever is heard often. It means you're screwed. She knows you are clueless to the situation, and she has lapsed into her read-my-mind mode. This simply means you are being given one last chance to save your nuts.

This is not a time to admit she is right or that you were wrong. This is a time to say those dreaded words every man hates hearing, "We need to talk." Sit down, preferably on a sofa or love seat. You sit on one end; she will sit on the other. Ask her to repeat the problem. This time instead of hearing blah, blah, blah, blah, blah, blah, blah, actually insert it with a word or two of what she is saying.

Example:

She says, "Blah, blah, blah, blah, blah! Blah, blah, blah, blab la blab maid?"

This translates into:

"Can't you pick up after yourself? Do I look like your maid?"

First, a word of wisdom. Never, ever, ever say yes to the maid question. Not even in jest. In fact, your best action is DO NOT SPEAK!

As she continues with the problem, and trust me she will, pretend to understand what she is saying. Slowly, I repeat slowly, move closer toward her. Maybe an inch and remember to protect your favorite man muscle in the process of this move. She is still upset with you. Let her keep talking. Give a nod and hang your head down low for a second or two. Then look up and deep into her eyes and slowly reach for her hand. This is when you go in for the kill.

You can say any one of the following:

1. "I do have things to work on, and that is something I am going to try to be better at."
2. "I am so grateful I have you."
3. "What can I do to help you?" (Then take notes!)

There is really no way to get out of this one except by cleaning up your act. Also, never brag about what you have done. This will piss her off big time then you will be back to *whatever*.

Why me is another W word. She is trying to understand why you are so clueless. She is taking all of the problems of marriage, from her point of view at least, on her shoulders. When you have reached the why me in a conversation, consider the fact you will not be having sex for the next month. This will be a good time to plan a romantic night for the two of you.

What's Wrong?

"What's wrong" is what you say. She in turn says, "Nothing." Unfortunately, the word *nothing*, not silence. Nothing is a dangerous word when it comes out of a woman's mouth. Again, we are going back to the reading of her mind. This is the time you need to recap the last twenty-four hours—everything you have done and said. This includes bathroom visits and breathing. Unfortunately, this is the calm before the storm. You have three options, and none of them may save you this time, but you will be prepared for the next time, and believe me there will be a next time.

1. "I have obviously done something wrong. Please tell me."
2. "I screw up so often we could be here all day long. Please tell me."
3. Drop to your knees and beg forgiveness

Words to avoid are "What?" and "Great. This again!"

Nothing also has another meaning, and it's very confusing either way.

He says, "What do you want for Christmas, birthday, anniversary?"
She says, "Nothing. You're all I need."

If you have a high or medium-maintenance woman, the word nothing means either of the following:

---

1. Jewelry
2. Flowers delivered at her work, if possible (birthday or anniversary)
3. Night of romance

Do not get her nothing, as in zero, nada, nothing. You will be in the doghouse for a long time, and she will never let you forget it. In fact, eighty years later, your tombstone may read "He got me nothing for my _____."

There are gifts to avoid if she is a high to medium-maintenance woman:

1. Vacuum
2. Blender
3. Can opener
4. Any kitchen appliance
5. Lawn mower
6. Weed wacker. This can cause permanent damage to your favorite man muscle.
7. Magazine subscription

This list is endless. Stick with jewelry. It is usually safe. A necklace is great. Maybe something in a heart shape. Pay attention to what type of jewelry she wears—silver or gold. If you are in doubt, go through her jewelry box. This doesn't need to be extravagant in price. If you can afford a $20.00 necklace, great. If you can afford more, even better. Just remember, don't go into debt over gifts you give her. Debt will also become your fault sooner or later.

Women tend to have their own language when it comes to communication. Some of those words are ones you also use; however, the meaning is totally different.

Time

Time to a woman can often be considered endless. When she says, "five minutes," sit back and relax. The next five minutes will be about an hour.

When you say five minutes during football or basketball game, she will hold you to it. Either way, you're screwed.

Thanks

Believe it or not, women do say thank you. All you need to say is "you're welcome." Anything else can get you in trouble.

If she says, "thanks a lot," she is not thanking you for doing a good thing. She is being totally sarcastic, and thanks a lot can mean many things. For example:

1. The sink is full of dirty dishes, and you left them for her. You could have avoided this entire situation by just doing the dishes, but now you're in hot water.
2. You leave your clothes and/or towel on the floor, and she picks up after you. Avoid the entire situation and pick up after yourself, AND DO NOT, I REPEAT DO NOT, praise yourself for doing so.
3. Hang up your coat.

Do I need to give any more examples? Just remember, the more you do around the house, the less you will hear "thanks a lot."

The F word

No, not that word. Get your mind out of the gutter. The word is *fine*. When a woman ends a conversation with this four-letter word, the discussion is over. You have three options in this situation:

1. Shut up
2. Shut up
3. Shut up

Anything else is wrong.

Living with a woman is hard enough, but for a week to ten days during the month, we are far from a joy to live with. There are certain phrases you need to avoid. By avoiding these, you will live long enough to have another joyous month next month:

1. "I know how you feel."
2. "It can't be all that bad."
3. "Get over it."
4. "Take it like a man."
5. "Choose something from your fat wardrobe."
6. "Wanna screw around anyway."
7. "You timed this one perfect."
8. "Not again."
9. "Blah, blah, blah, blah, blah."
10. "You did this on purpose."

11. "How many more years do I have to deal with this?" (Avoid this phrase at all cost.)

The Thing You Can Say

Nothing

Every word that comes out of your mouth is wrong. However, this is the perfect time to pick up your clothes, hang up your coat, vacuum, dust, and do dishes. When she asks you to go to the store because she needs "a few things," be a man and listen to what she wants and get it exactly. If she has a box of tampons, cut out the label and don't screw up. You sex life, whenever you have one again, will depend on it. Also, consider this a blessing in disguise. You get to escape out of the house for about an hour.

Enjoy these special moments.

Now that you've been given fair warning on how to deal with some problems, let me help you avoid problems.

1. Flowers

Flowers are a beautiful gift of love unless your wife is allergic, then not so good. Never purchase flowers when you are in the doghouse. Buy them before you get there. You do not need to spend a lot of money. Most grocery stores carry flowers now. You don't need to get a fancy bouquet that will run you $50.00 plus dollars. Simple flowers will do. Twice a month is good. If she is not watching her weight, a small box of chocolates is nice.

If you go to a florist, use the same one on a regular basis. This helps your local economy, and you will become the great husband you think you are in someone's eyes, not the one you married but someone's.

2. A Night of Romance

Women enjoy romance. Set a date. Clear it with her first and give her only one detail: "I have a special night planned for the both of us." This is all she needs to know. Mail her a reminder note a few days before.

NOTE: Be romantic.
I'm looking forward to our date on _____.
I love you.

Check ahead for any movie she would like to see. It will probably be a chick flick. Bring a clean cloth handkerchief not a paper towel. You can purchase these

—

at most Wal-Marts, K-Marts, or Sears. Go to the men's department and ask for help. Just get it over with. When she begins to sniffle, bring it out of your suit pocket. Yes, suit and tie are required for a romantic evening, and when she starts to cry periodically, wipe the side of your eye. There will probably will be no tears on your part, just pretend to wipe a few times during the movie. Women enjoy this side of a man. Also pay attention to the movie, there will be a quiz afterward.

If she has a favorite restaurant you like to frequent, call ahead for a special table. Even better, go in and talk to the boss. Prepare ahead and have flowers ready for her. Enjoy romance; it's not as bad as you think. The best part of a romantic night is you get the reward: sex.

There will be many things you forget during your marriage. The most important will be dates—wedding, birthdays (children included), anniversary, etc. This is a moment you can show your wife you do have emotions and possibly get another night of sex. Sit down with her and write a list of the dates you need through the calendar year. If you write this on an index card, you can keep it in your wallet. If she goes through your wallet, she will come across the list, and most women will be thrilled you at least try to keep track. Other women want you to memorize it. Those are usually the women that make a great ex-wife.

Sample:

> Special dates to remember
> My wonderful wife's birthday: _____
> Our wedding day: _____
> Her mother's birthday: _____
> My mother's birthday: _____
> Her father's birthday: _____
> My father's birthday: _____
> Children: _____

Insert names here. (Numbers are not an option.)

During your marriage, your wife will question you about the wedding day. Remember it was her day. Most husbands remember nothing. So when questioned remember this small, sweet answer:

"All I remember about that beautiful day (doesn't matter if it was pouring down rain) is how beautiful my bride was. Nothing else was important."

This may sound sappy, and if you think you are too tough of a macho man to say this, think again. Part of marriage is sometimes telling your wife things that will make her happy. It's not a bad thing. It's just one of those things you would say when you escape out of a bathroom window. For example:

When she asks "Does this dress make me look fat?"

Never let her finish the sentence. When she is looking at the mirror tell her how beautiful she is. As soon as she speaks those words, you are in trouble. Deep trouble.

The reading of a woman's mind actually began with Adam and Eve. The rib bone that was removed from Adam in order to form Eve had a unique quality. It had the blessed gift that gave man the ability to read a woman's mind. Unfortunately when it was removed and given to Eve she was given the gift of reading a man's mind and unfortunately Adam, and generations to come did not come with the gift. Men now you know why you are totally clueless when it comes to understanding women.

My husband remembers nothing about our wedding except that I wore a white dress and that I too prompt him on. One of my best friends, Karla Matson, sang at our wedding. Karla has a beautiful voice that draws you into every note she sings. It's as if she is singing just for you and no one else is in the room. She was obviously singing to everyone except my husband because they remember her. She is a constant professional, and it's no wonder she lives in Branson, Missouri the county music capital of the mid-west. Even though my wonderful husband remembers nothing of the wedding, he does have wonderfully clear memories of the honeymoon. Most husbands do. Imagine that?

Marriage will never be easy, but it is worth it. It is a beautiful time of your life as it is also a pain in the butt. Never assume your friends don't have the same problems with their spouse because you will always find someone's spouse who is worse than yours.

However, just remember men and women are different. As humans, we have good qualities and bad. If by chance you go into an abusive relationship, run for the hills. Once a man hits, he will never stop. Seek help and never blame yourself. You are not the one with the problem. He is.

With all hope, you have gained a bit of wisdom through the pages of this book. I ask only one thing of you and that is to remember this:

Marriage is a sacred covenant between a man and a woman. Neither party should rush into a marital union, especially when one party is not sure. When there are problems, use patience, compassion and love. Remember the vows you made on your wedding day. Together the two of you will have a commitment that will influence generations to come.

Or

Men and women put their pants on the same way.
What makes us unique is how they come off.